# GHOSTS OF
# SOUTH WALES

# GHOSTS
# OF
# SOUTH WALES

Steve Lockley

COUNTRYSIDE BOOKS
NEWBURY, BERKSHIRE

Cover illustration by Colin Doggett

Produced through MRM Associates Ltd., Reading
Printed by J. W. Arrowsmith Ltd., Bristol

# INTRODUCTION

LET me start with a confession. I have never seen a ghost although I have spoken to many people who say they have, and in most cases I have little difficulty in being convinced that they are telling me exactly what they saw.

The closest I have ever come to a similar experience could easily be put down to a rampant imagination at a time of high anxiety. On the night after my grandmother died, when I was in my early teens, I was lying awake for hours unable to sleep. The rest of the family had gone to bed and the house was quiet apart from the sound of settling floorboards which happens in older houses. Then, in the middle of the silence, a rocking chair in the corner of my room creaked not once but twice. Rather than becoming agitated by this I felt more at ease and fell asleep. The chair had been given to me by my grandmother.

When I first started to research this book I had somehow thought that there would be a wealth of material to draw on which would send shivers down the spine. While I was not disappointed with the eerie quality of some of the stories I tracked down, there was far from the volume of material I had anticipated.

A number of excellent books already existed and I used these as my starting point, but in several libraries I visited I discovered more books on hauntings in England than in the Principality which supports them. Was Wales actually a place less troubled by restless spirits than other parts of the British Isles, or were the recipients of visitations in Wales simply less willing to talk about their experiences?

As I started to pull the stories together it became apparent that a significant number of them have

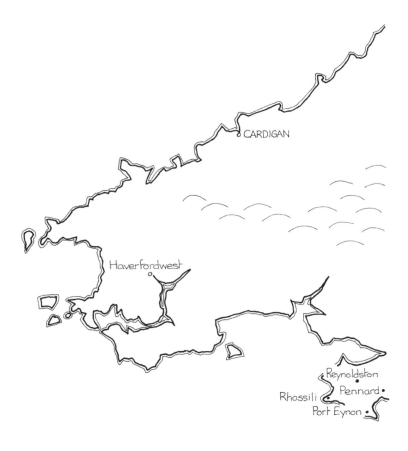

CARDIGAN

Haverfordwest

Reynoldston

Pennard

Rhossili

Port Eynon

# Ghosts of
# South Wales

Llanfihangel
Crucorney

Abergavenny

Craig-y-Nos •

Nantyglo •

Llanellan
Monmouth •

MERTHYR
TYDFIL •

EBBW
VALE

• Glyncorrwg

Mountain
• Ash

Usk •

Tintern
Abbey •

SWANSEA

o NEATH
PORT
TALBOT

Cwmbran •

Chepstow

The
Mumbles

• Llangynwyd

• Margam

Caerphilly
•

Caerleon

NEWPORT

PORTHCAWL •

Tongwynlais

Cowbridge •

Llandaff

CARDIFF

Southerndown

• Llanvithyn

Welsh St Donats

St Athan

Llantwit
Major

Swanbridge

grown out of a folklore which is now firmly rooted. In fact it is clear that many locals seem to associate any strange behaviour with these old legends. Some stories are well documented from a not too distant past when perhaps people were more open minded about ghosts and were perfectly happy to talk freely about their strange experiences. The other, more recent, hauntings may be fewer in number, but I clearly detected a reticence among those involved to discuss what they had witnessed. It was almost as if they thought that despite events having been reported in the newspapers they were still holding themselves up to be ridiculed.

In order to help make sense of some of the stories derived from legend I have included at the end of this book a short section on aspects of Welsh supernatural lore, in particular those dreaded omens of impending disaster.

The stories here will I hope entertain, but also leave that cold shiver – as if someone is perhaps reading over your shoulder.

This book would not have been completed without the influence of four people, and to each I owe a debt of gratitude. Firstly to David Bell, who has already contributed a number of titles to this series, and is responsible for putting the idea in my head; to David Graves of Countryside Books who badgered me until I finished it; to Paul Lewis for help with some of the bits in between by providing occasional help with research; and also to my wife Elaine for putting up with me disappearing for hours on end while I tapped away on the word processor.

Steve Lockley

# ABERGAVENNY

## The Haunted Doll's House

IN 1992 a new Toy Museum opened in the town of Abergavenny. One of its prized exhibits was possibly the smallest haunted house on record, a haunted doll's house.

The house has a well travelled history. Having been built in Germany in the 1880s, it was taken to America by a German immigrant. It remained in the same family until 1910 when it was sold. Some 30 or so years later it was bought by a mining engineer from Merthyr Tydfil who was working and living with his wife and his son and daughter in the United States.

When the family returned to Merthyr the father stayed behind in order to complete his contract and was due to follow the rest of them home six months later. One day the daughter claimed to have seen her father inside the doll's house. Her mother dismissed the idea as a product of the girl's imagination but the child continued with her assertions that her father had waved to her from one of the windows.

Shortly after this episode the family received a visit from representatives of the father's employers who had called to tell them that the ship he had been travelling on had been torpedoed by a German U-boat. The family were naturally devastated. Soon after this the rest of the family perished in a house fire, but the doll's house remained strangely unharmed.

In due course the doll's house fell into the hands of a family from Cilfynydd. The children of the new family claimed that they had seen two other children, a boy and a girl, waving to them from one of the windows.

This story was related on BBC Radio Wales at the

time of the museum's opening and perhaps this publicity stimulated visitors' imaginations, but dozens of people have now also claimed to have seen things through the windows of this intriguing doll's house.

# CAERLEON

### The Army of the Dead

DURING the occupation of Britain by the Romans, two legions were stationed in Wales. One of these was in the town of Chester, while the other was based at Caerleon-on-Usk near Newport. This was the Second Augustan Legion, a body of 5,500 troops which were quartered at the 50 acre fortress that had been established in AD 75.

The remains of the fortress, the baths and the amphitheatre can still be visited and are quite an attraction for the area. It is the amphitheatre in particular that is of the greatest interest to ghost hunters. Perhaps it is merely the atmosphere generated by the place that causes a leap of imagination or perhaps the ghosts of Roman soldiers remain as, from time to time, there can still be heard the ghostly sound of footsteps.

Another possible explanation for the sound of footsteps could be a phenomenon which was quite widely reported in the Middle Ages in mainland Europe, and was recorded in various parts of Hereford and the Marches in the 12th century.

The Herlethingi, the army of the dead, were seen at noon. These long-dead soldiers marched with carts, horses and other paraphernalia of war, shouting and trumpeting. They have not been seen in modern times but there have been occasions when the noise of their passing has been heard even if they have remained invisible.

The atmosphere of this place has certainly had an effect on more than one person and may indeed have been a contributing factor to the imagination of one of Wales' finest writers of supernatural and fantastic fiction. Caerleon-on-Usk was the birthplace of the celebrated Arthur Machen.

# CAERPHILLY

## A Haunted Farmhouse

ON the outskirts of the town of Caerphilly, where the houses give way to grim mountains, and sheep become more frequent than people, there stands a farmhouse that was once more troubled by the dead than the living. Within months of the property having been built and the farmer and his wife having moved in, the noises began. At night when all around was as silent as the grave, one room in this lonely house was alive with enough noise to wake more than the sleeping. Eventually the farmer and his wife felt they had no choice but to discuss their problems with the local priest.

The priest was sceptical about the couple's assertions, but as the troubles had forced them out of their home in search of sleep, he offered to spend the night in the house. After the farmer and his wife had left their home to stay with family, the priest settled himself beside the fire to read.

It was in the early hours of the morning, with the fire burnt down to embers and the house becoming cold, that the priest was woken by the sound of knocking. For several moments he remained in the chair, startled by the noise and by waking up in unfamiliar surroundings. As he came to his senses the knocking became louder and with it he began to pick out the sound of a plaintive voice calling.

After lighting the fresh candle he had kept at his side for this purpose he followed the sound of the knocking, holding out his leather-bound bible to ward off evil. When he swung the door open and looked inside the room, the noise was almost unbearable, as the banging against one wall beat out a deafening tattoo. There, in the shadowy light the candle provided, he could make out the translucent figure of a boy, floating halfway up the wall, hammering for all he was worth.

'What do you want?' said the priest, no longer afraid at the sight. 'What in the name of God do you want?'

The boy ignored him, choosing – or compelled – to continue with his efforts, until the priest could make out his cries. 'Let me out. Let me out,' he was calling over and over again.

With that the door slammed closed in front of the priest, causing a draught which extinguished the candle. The banging stopped, and when the priest reopened the door the room was empty. He then returned to his chair by the remaining warmth of the fire and fell asleep once more.

Later the banging started again, but by now the sun had risen. The priest was relieved to find that the noise was coming not from the room where he had seen the ghostly figure, but the back door. The farmer and his wife had returned but were unwilling to re-enter the house until they were sure that the priest was safe.

'I think I know what the problem is,' said the priest, 'but to cure it may not be pleasant. It would be a good idea if you asked a neighbour to help.'

Later that morning, before the priest had taken breakfast – and he was glad of it – he re-entered the room with the farmer and his neighbour. It took half an hour to break through the wall where the ghost had been beating, and as they did the pent up odours made it almost unbearable to continue. When finally they had broken through what it soon became obvious was a false wall they found the decayed remains of a boy. Once the body had been taken away to be afforded the right of Christian burial the farmhouse became at peace.

The boy, it transpired, had been apprenticed to the mason charged with building the house and he had been murdered and his body hidden behind the wall while the property was being built.

## Troubled Spirits at Caerphilly Castle

THE de Clare family have secured themselves a special place in the history of Wales, certainly as far as the south-east corner is concerned, where many of their ancestral homes are still standing. Tintern Abbey was built by Walter de Clare, but it is Caerphilly Castle, which was built by Gilbert de Clare who was known as the 'Red Earl', that has become perhaps the prime abode of some of the spirits of the long departed. It was also a de Clare who suffered at the hands of Sir Jasper Berkerolles of West Orchard, near St Athan.

Caerphilly Castle was built in the 13th century and

13

yet remains remarkably intact. It is reputedly haunted by at least three troubled spirits.

The first soul in torment is thought to be that of Gilbert's French wife, Alice. On discovering that she had been having an affair, Gilbert banished her to France where she spent the rest of her life. It was not until after her death that she finally had the opportunity to return. She now wanders the castle, having regained her home.

The second is assumed to be another member of the de Clare family. A number of sightings have been made of a ghostly figure in full armour. Appearances of this particular spirit appear to be limited to the castle ramparts.

The third spirit has provided a far more terrifying sight, a Gwrach y Rhibyn. She is said to have red eyes set into an over-large head. She wears a tight fitting green dress covered by a cloak, which she uses to flap around the castle walls after she emerges from the murky waters of the castle moat.

# CARDIFF

### Gentle Spirits at Cardiff Castle

THE history of Cardiff Castle is a long and bloody one, and yet the spirits which are said to inhabit it and the surrounding lands do not provide a reflection of this violent past.

A major restoration of the castle was started in the first half of the 19th century by its then owner, John Crichton Stuart, the second Marquis of Bute. The prosperity of Cardiff itself owes much to the Marquis, who invested a great deal of his wealth in creating the docks to export Welsh coal around the world.

Sadly the Marquis died in his private dressing room and did not see the fulfilment of his dream, at least during his lifetime, but his son continued the work his father had started. It does appear, however, that such was the father's love of the place that the Marquis' spirit has been unable to leave.

The ghost of the Marquis is said to appear in the library after walking through the large fireplace there. He then leaves the room by passing through a wall which is six feet thick and built of solid stone. Reappearing in the corridor on the other side, he then goes through the wall of the chapel which his son built in his memory and into the dressing room where he died. At precisely 3.45 am, heavy doors have been known to open and close by themselves.

Other apparitions include a 'faceless vision in flowing white skirts' which has been seen in this part of the castle and also in the nearby stockroom. Apparently she is known by the name of Sarah and any disturbance created by her stops when her name is called out in anger.

A Grey Lady haunts the bridge over the river Taff which runs close by. She is seen to be waving towards the castle, and local legend has it that she is waving to Duke Robert of Normandy, who was the eldest son of William the Conqueror. Robert was held captive for 28 years in the wooden keep which preceded the present structure. Sadly it is unlikely that he would be able to see the Grey Lady, having been blinded by his captors.

A phantom coach used to haunt the castle at the time the Bute family lived there. They left in 1948, but before that the coach was said to appear whenever there was an impending death in the family.

## The Ghost That Took Offence

OPENED in 1922, the National Museum of Wales stands near to Cardiff Castle in the city centre, and is said to be haunted by its architect, Dunbar Smith. After his death, Smith's ashes were sealed in a casket in the central block of the museum but in more recent years it has been moved to a less auspicious resting place close to the gents' toilets. Smith's ghost appears to have taken umbrage at this and is being held responsible for a number of strange happenings which have occurred in various parts of the building. These range from lifts starting to move without being summoned, a television set switching itself on after the cleaners have left and a chair which is constantly being moved in the night, to a more direct manifestation. One of the attendants has seen the ghost itself.

One night the attendant was checking the archaeology department to ensure that all the visitors had left. Having found no one there he started to leave the area in order to carry on with his rounds but something made him stop and turn around. There, where there had been no one before, was a tall, thin man dressed in black standing in front of one of the display cases. The figure then disappeared.

The attendant managed to collect his thoughts, despite the fright he had just received, and he completed a thorough search of the area, but there was no one there.


## The New Theatre Ghost

CARDIFF'S New Theatre is said to be haunted by the ghost of an old lady who has been seen at fairly regular intervals over the years. She appears at first in one of the theatre's boxes, where she seems to be looking for something. She then leaves the box and starts to walk down the stairs to the stalls. From there she disappears once more.

While there does not appear to be any proof to support the theory, it has long been thought that perhaps she is the ghost of a woman who fell from the box during a matinee performance.

Some time ago in the same theatre, an electrician was focusing a spotlight onto the stage when he lost his balance. For an instant he felt that he was doomed to fall. To his relief he then felt someone grab hold of his leg to save him from injuries that could easily have proved fatal. When he turned to thank whoever had saved him, he was shocked to find that there was no one there.

On another occasion, the stage manager saw a door to the circle area open, seemingly of its own accord. Another time he felt a sudden drop in temperature when the rest of the theatre was warm. He also sensed some sort of a presence nearby.

Major renovations to the theatre were completed in 1988. While such work is often accompanied by an increase in spectral activity, this has not been so with the New Theatre. There have been no further sightings of the old lady, nor reports of anyone experiencing anything similar to that felt by the stage manager.


## Cardiff's Most Haunted Building?

CATHEDRAL ROAD runs through the Pontcanna district of Cardiff. If all the stories about a single building on that road are to be believed, then, with the possible exception of Cardiff Castle, it is the most haunted building in the capital.

The building in question was at one time the offices of the Automobile Association, and although they have always officially dismissed any notion of the building being haunted, many of the staff who have worked there have reported sightings. Two ghosts in particular are recorded as making regular appearances.

The first ghost is that of a woman who was seen so regularly by the staff that they even gave her a name. They called her 'Alice'. Her hair was always tied back in a bun, accommodating a pair of old fashioned earphones, and she wore a shabby dress.

Her appearances have been reported as often being heralded by an evil smell. When seen, Alice would smile sweetly before disappearing. Others say that this was not a sweet smile at all, but an evil grin revealing all her teeth.

The building was once part of a convent, and it is not surprising therefore that the second ghostly figure is that of a nun. She is usually spotted on the top floor, but pays no attention to whoever sees her.

These two ghosts only scratch the surface of reported hauntings associated with the premises. For example, a phantom cat has been seen in a flat adjoining the offices – passing through walls unhindered.

There is also a long history of poltergeist activity, which ranges from the mundane rearrangement of furniture and doors slamming to the hurtling of chairs through the air. One woman who lived in the flat went to turn on the heater one evening only to have a ghostly hand materialise alongside her own. Her husband was out at work that evening but she left the flat and refused to return.

## An Endless Torment at Penylan Well

IN the early part of the 19th century, Penylan Well was said to be haunted by a ghostly Lady in Black who was seen regularly beside the well itself. On each occasion she appeared she would be wailing and moaning, obviously in distress. Rather than eliciting sympathy from whoever saw her, she only succeeded in frightening them. This naturally caused everyone to give her, and the well, a wide berth.

Eventually, one man who was unafraid of the apparition stopped and tried to talk to her in the hope that he might be able to ease her torment. Although the ghost did not confide in the man what the cause or nature of her distress was, she told him that there was a way in which he could help her. If she was to be freed from her torment he should hold her tightly around her waist and not release her, no matter what he should see or feel.

I do not know how on earth it is possible to take hold of an apparition, but the man complied with her request and used his arms to encircle her waist. As soon he did so he felt a sharp, unbearable, stabbing pain in his arm which forced him to loosen his grip. Despite his best efforts not to fail in his promise he was unable to maintain his hold.

In the instant that the man released her, the Lady in Black disappeared screaming into the distance. As she faded away she swore at him, saying that he had failed her. She also cried that it would now take another 200 years before she could be freed.

# CARDIGAN

## A Phantom Funeral

THE harvest in 1816 in Wales was one of the wettest on record and so every dry moment was seized in order to carry out work in the fields. It was therefore quite late one evening that a Cardiganshire farmer and his wife were binding sheaves from corn which was already cut and lying on the ground. The evening was dry, as the day had been, and thanks to a clear sky and a full moon there was sufficient light to work by.

The main road through the parish ran along one edge of the field with neither a hedge nor a ditch separating it from the crop. After they had been working for half an hour or so they heard the hum of deep voices as if a crowd of people was approaching them along the road. They paused in their work and saw a host of men and women coming into sight and heading their way.

Being intent on getting as much of the work done as they could before they were too tired to continue they bent their backs again to the task, without paying any more attention to what was happening on the road. When they next looked up they saw that the amongst the crowd of late night walkers was carried a coffin. They then watched the procession until after it had passed them, almost oblivious to the fact that funerals were never conducted at night.

They found themselves unable to take their eyes off the crowd until it had drawn level with them and they saw that although most of the men and women were walking on the road, many strayed onto the field and were treading on the corn. The sound of voices continued, but despite the fact that they were only a matter of yards away and it was a clear, quiet night they were unable to make out as much as a syllable of their speech. Nor did they recognise a single face in the crowd.

The procession then walked on along the road away from them and towards the parish church. The couple were left with a very disconcerted feeling and despite their desire to continue working they decided to go home. When they returned to their work early the following morning they were surprised that there was not a single footprint at the side of the road where the night before some of the mourners had walked through the corn.

A tailor who was walking along the road further along from the field also met the procession – at a point where it was bounded by a hedge on either side. The mourners filled the road from side to side and despite the tailor's best efforts he was unable to find a way through. In fact the force of the crowd was such that he was pushed backwards until he was obliged to climb over the hedge to avoid the flow of people who seemed ignorant of his presence.

There was no funeral that night. It was no more than a ghostly rehearsal for one which took the same route three weeks later.

# CHEPSTOW

### The Grey Lady at the Golf Club

THE St Pierre Country Club at Chepstow was once a stately home, but is now a prestigious golf club.

The house was visited by Henry V when Sir David ap Phillip was Lord of St Pierre. Sir David fought for both Henry IV and Henry V in the wars against the French. Henry V also chose to hide his jewels in the walls of the first floor of the tower before his death, and they remained there for some time until they were handed over to Henry VI.

David ap Phillip's son took the family name of Lewis rather than being known by the Welsh tradition (ap meaning 'son of') and eventually became Governor of Calais. The Lewis family remained occupants of the property for several generations.

The house is home to a Grey Lady who is said to be a member of the Lewis family whose favours were fought over in a duel. There have also been a number of strange noises and inexplicable happenings in the house, most of which first started being reported in the 1950s.

# COWBRIDGE

### The Grey Man at Caercady House

CAERCADY HOUSE stands between Welsh St Donats and the village of Prisk, and during the 19th century it was said to be haunted by at least one ghost, who it appears became almost a part of the family.

The family who owned the house complained of the sound of knocking coming from the floors, and of hearing the rustle of long dresses. They also heard the sound of heavy footsteps on the stairs and of something heavy being dropped onto the floor of one of the upstairs rooms. After that particular noise it would sound as if books were being scattered across the floor, sliding across the bare floorboards.

They also became very used to the sound of knocking at both the front and back doors, but whenever they went to answer the door there was never anyone there. Eventually they decided to ignore the knocking no matter how persistent it became, and before long they saw the ghostly figure of a man dressed in grey with what they described as a disappointed look on his face.

From then on they referred to this particular spirit as the Grey Man and it appears that they grew quite comfortable with his presence. An explanation for the sound of rustling dresses has never been suggested.

# CRAIG-Y-NOS

## The Tylwyth Teg Guard Their Treasure

ONCE the home of the world renowned Edwardian opera singer Adelina Patti, the castle of Craig-y-Nos stands high in the Swansea valley. From time to time the house and its gardens have been open as a tourist attraction but it now seems to receive a high proportion of its visitors through the regular antique fairs held there. Long ago many people who lived in the general area of Craig-y-Nos claimed that it entertained more strange and sinister guests.

Legend has it that many generations before the time of Adelina Patti, the Tylwyth Teg (fairy folk) stored their treasure in a large cave, or perhaps a tunnel, that ran beneath Craig-y-Nos. To reach the castle the fairies climbed the high walls with the aid of a ladder which was made of 20 rungs of pure gold. Once the fairies had attained the castle courtyard they would approach a massive slab of stone which hid the entrance to their treasure trove. When they spoke secret passwords the slab would slide aside to let them enter, much like the entrance to Ali Baba's cave.

Being well aware of the talk of the fairies' treasure, a young shepherd watched their activity for several nights. Having seen the way in which they climbed their golden ladder he decided to hide in wait for them inside the courtyard. It was his intention to try to learn the passwords that would let him into their hoard.

He waited through the evening, huddling himself into the shadowy corners beneath the castle walls for fear that he might be seen, such was his terror of the Tylwyth Teg. This was despite the fact that he knew that the tiny folk would not appear until after midnight. Shortly after the strike of twelve the first figure appeared at last, carrying a tiny sack on its shoulder. At first the shepherd could not make out the words the fairy spoke, but as one after another used the passwords he learnt them by heart.

Early the next afternoon he returned to the castle, and standing beside the slab that he had seen slide open he repeated the same words himself. The stone slid aside exactly as it had done the night before and he made his way inside. Within minutes he found himself in darkness on the steps that led down into the treasure room as the slab had closed behind him without warning. In his panic he spoke the words again in order that he might leave and return later, but this time with a means of lighting his way.

Imagine his shock when he discovered that despite repeating the words perfectly over and over again, each time with growing desperation, the slab refused to move. He needed different passwords to get out.

His presence was detected by the fairy folk almost as soon as they returned that night, and for seven years they held him captive until he was fortunate enough to learn the passwords which allowed him to leave the castle. He was then able to make good his escape. Soon after his return to the world outside his prison he told a friend, who was a local farmer, of his ordeal. The farmer offered to give the shepherd a share of the treasure in exchange for the passwords, and although the shepherd was reluctant at first he finally agreed. The farmer succeeded in getting in and out of the castle with a small amount of treasure at first without detection but as he grew in confidence he returned again and again. Eventually he succumbed to greed and went back on one occasion too many.

The fairies caught him, as easily as they had the shepherd, but this time were so angry at the violation of their treasure trove that rather than keep him prisoner they murdered him slowly and painfully. His remains were quartered and hung on hooks in one of the castle's cellars.

The tale of the fairies may well be a hard piece of folklore to take at face value but in most local legends there is some grain of truth behind the embellishments. One view is that perhaps this tale was created in order to cover up the murder of a thief by one of the castle servants.

Some of the older residents in the area around Craig-y-Nos claim that on quiet nights strange noises can be heard coming from the castle. They say it is possible to hear the ghost of the greedy farmer, who still rattles the iron hooks where he had hung, and his voice echoes up the valley screaming 'Let me live, let me live.'

# CWMBRAN

### The Pool of Avarice

IN the hills that stand above the town of Cwmbran lies a dark, dank pool choked with weeds. The stretch of water is known as the Pool of Avarice as a reminder of an event in its history which changed not only its physical landscape but also removed any signs of habitation. There once stood a large house nearby, but there is now no trace of its existence.

One night as a storm was threatening to break over the mountains, the family in the house were preparing a lavish meal for a small group of friends. The feast had been talked about in the surrounding villages for days, and yet a number of less well off members of the family who lived in the area were excluded from the party. On hearing of the feast, one of these poor relatives called at the back door of the house begging for food for his family. The relative was turned away empty handed, even more humiliated then than he was by the lack of an invitation.

Shortly after this, while the relative was still making his way home without the treats he had hoped to be able to provide for his family, the storm broke.

This storm was worse then any witnessed in living memory, and the downpour was so torrential that part of Twyn Berllan, the mountain standing over the house, was washed away. The subsequent landslip thundered down the mountain at such a speed that there was no chance for anyone to make their escape. The destruction was so severe and complete that the house was buried in its entirety, leaving no survivors.

On similar stormy nights, it is said that the cries of the dead can be heard. The sound of their torment in punishment for their avarice echoes around the pool, as perhaps at last they regret their lack of charity.

# EBBW VALE

### The Mill Stream Ghost

IN Ebbw Vale during the reign of Queen Victoria, a young girl fell in love with the son of a wealthy farmer. Unfortunately, for her at least, her lover's parents were determined to keep them apart, intent on their son marrying the daughter of a sea captain friend of theirs. Despite their objections, the pair continued to meet in secret.

The farmer's son, perhaps to keep the girl happy, or more likely to secure her 'favours', married her on the condition that the fact be kept secret. The marriage was bogus, being conducted by a friend of the farmer's son who had agreed to pose as a clergyman.

Shortly after the 'marriage' the man began to become indifferent to her, and called to see her less and less. Finally he stopped seeing her altogether – before she was able to tell him that she was pregnant.

The child was born, and the girl's father threatened to turn her out of the house for shaming the family by bringing a child into the world while still unmarried. The girl broke down in tears and told him about her marriage to the farmer's son. The father then called on the farmer and demanded that the son should stand by his daughter. It was then that the truth of the sham marriage came out.

Despite this revelation, the girl's father still insisted that the young man should be a husband to his daughter and a father to the child, but the farmer would have none of it. He continued to say that his son was to marry the sea captain's daughter.

Shortly before the wedding the girl met her errant lover at the mill stream where they had spent much of their time together. She had hoped to persuade him to change his mind, and to this end she took the baby with her. He had never seen the child and the girl thought that seeing the baby might force him to reconsider.

On the following day the bodies of the girl and the baby were found floating in the stream. Had she committed suicide and taken her child's life with her after a failed attempt at reconciliation? Or had they been drowned by the farmer's son? The answer is not known.

The marriage with the sea captain's daughter went ahead, but ended before they had seen the honeymoon out when the farmer's son died in an accident. The irony of the story is that he thus left his wife alone while expecting his baby just as he had his former lover.

The ghost of the dead girl has been seen on several occasions wandering beside the mill stream. She still holds her baby to her chest.

# GLYNCORRWG

## The Bakehouse Ghost

DURING the 1930s, at the height of the depression, an unemployed baker arrived at Glyncorrwg, a small village to the north of Maesteg. As he had been unable to find work in his home town of Llangollen in North Wales he had decided to travel to the south of the country having secured a job at the Glyncorrwg bakery. Within days of starting the job, however, he had left his new found employment and returned home.

Shortly after deserting his position he was called before the Court of References in Wrexham. The baker was being threatened with having his unemployment benefit withdrawn for leaving his new employment voluntarily, but was being given the opportunity to state his case before the court. The loss of benefit would not only have brought poverty, but could also have blighted his chances of future employment, particularly in such difficult times.

He explained to the court that his first night in the bakery had passed without incident, but on the second night he had been distracted from his work when he heard a tapping sound at one of the windows. The time was shortly after midnight and, being unable to see anything through the window, he went around the side of the building outside to investigate. By the time he had made his way outside the noise had stopped. In the dark he was unable to find anything that could have caused the tapping. Being more confused than concerned, he had returned inside to continue with his work, but shortly after this the tapping started again and continued relentlessly, this time for almost an hour.

When the baker went into work on the third night he was already starting to feel more than a little uneasy about the place, but began to carry out his duties. Throughout the night he found himself keeping one eye on the window, and although he expected the noise to start again it did not. During the shift, however, he felt a sudden draught as if someone had walked past him. This incident alone was enough to send a shiver down his spine, but this was not to be the end of the matter.

On the fourth and final night of the baker's employment in Glyncorrwg came the culmination of these events. An incident occurred which convinced him that the building was haunted and he felt he was left with no choice but to return home to Llangollen. As he worked he heard noises coming from a room connected to the bakehouse. He ignored them at first, but as they became louder and more insistent he decided to investigate. When he opened the door he was confronted by an old woman wearing a black dress. The figure seemed to float past him into the bakehouse, looked at him and disappeared.

No one would have been surprised if after giving this statement he had been laughed out of the court, but this was far from the case. The owner of the bakery, instead of feeling betrayed by his employee deserting him, expressed a certain amount of sympathy and supported his testimony. He reported that over the years a number of his employees had told him of similar experiences. They too had heard strange noises at night, including a tapping at the window, and several had seen the old lady in black.

While the baker did not escape totally without punishment, his unemployment benefit was stopped for only one week. This was certainly a case of mitigating circumstances.

## A Woman in White at the Mine

DESPITE the small size of Glyncorrwg, certainly at the time of this occurrence, the village also boasts a second ghost. As with the events at Morfa Colliery at Taibach (see p. 68), the mine which once operated at Glyncorrwg also had a recorded history of ghostly warnings. The underground tunnels of the colliery were said to be haunted by a Woman in White, and sight of her was supposed to be the sign of impending disaster.

In July 1902, the lady was seen by a miner in one of the remote tunnels, waving her arms above her head. Other miners also heard the sound of blood-curdling screams echoing through the tunnels in other parts of mine. The sighting and the eerie screams led to over 300 miners refusing to go underground at the start of the following shift.

Unlike the devastation which followed the warnings given at Morfa, there was no disaster that night. But who is to say whether or not there would have been one had the men decided to leave the warning unheeded and go in to work?

# HAVERFORDWEST

## A Time of Unrest

THIS tale of the haunting of the castle at Haverfordwest takes us a little further west than most of the stories included in this volume and serves to demonstrate the hatred that the Welsh once held for the English invaders.

Haverfordwest is the capital of Landsker, also known as 'Little England beyond Wales'. The castle was originally built by an earlier group of incomers, the Normans, but their willingness to intermarry made it much easier for them to break down many of the barriers which were brought up.

In later years, at a time of unrest among the locals, the English Governor of the castle had taken a Welsh brigand captive. He had both tortured and blinded the man in order to gain the names of the other men involved in the uprising but the man would not talk. The Governor, perhaps out of remorse for his actions, then kept the man imprisoned within the castle, rather than having him killed. The Welshman was, however, allowed to move fairly freely within the building.

The Governor's young son used to talk to the prisoner and revelled in the tales he told, but the Welshman never forgot who he was or how he had been treated. One day he grabbed the boy and used him as a shield as he made his way up to the battlements. The Governor begged that his son's life be spared but the Welshman showed no mercy, throwing the boy over the castle walls before jumping to his own death.

From time to time there have been reports of ghostly movements in the castle, and it would be quite easy to attribute these to the Welshman who is paying penance for the murder of a small boy.

# LLANDAFF

## A Quartet of Ghosts

ONCE a small village in its own right, Llandaff has now been swallowed up into the environs of the city of Cardiff. The village green remains, as do several ancient buildings which include the ruins of an old priory. A number of ghost stories exist concerning the village, including three which involve the river Taff which flows nearby.

The first ghost is that of a grief-stricken woman who haunts the bank of the river and the grounds of Cardiff Cathedral which stands close by. The woman is thought to be a mother whose only son was drowned in the river, but whose body was never found. The ghost paces up and down, still looking for him.

The second is a ghost known as Bella who is believed to have been the wife of the landlord of an inn which used to stand in Llandaff. During her life-time she discovered religion and turned against the drinking, gambling and other vices which took place at her husband's establishment. One night she argued with him and in rage ran out to the river and threw herself in. Her ghost now haunts the river bank too.

The third ghost is the strangely named 'Frog Lady of Llandaff'. The woman came from a well-respected village family but owing to both physical and mental handicap she spent her lifetime moving around in a frog-like, hopping motion. The parents put their daughter out for adoption to the family of an agricultural labourer. One night, she fell into the river and drowned, and her ghost is now said to appear on certain moonlit nights in the area around the weir.

The Maltsters Arms is also said to be the home of a ghost. In 1965 the landlord of the time, Ken Perrett, reported that he had seen the shape of a small, dark man wandering through the bar during the night.

# LLANELLAN

## The White Lady of the Village of the Dead

TO the east of the village of Llanrhidian on the Gower peninsula is the site of the long lost village of Llanellan, also known as the village of the dead. Now there is only a farm acting as a marker for the site.

Long ago a ship was beached in the estuary, but its crew and passengers were fortunate enough to be able to climb from the vessel and reach the shore. From there they made their way on up the hill until they reached the village of Llanellan. While shipwrecks were not uncommon along that particular stretch of coastline, it was rare for survivors to make it as far as Llanellan. In a spirit of charity and hospitality the villagers made their visitors welcome.

Within days of their arrival it became apparent that the villagers had made a dreadful mistake as one by one all of the survivors began to show symptoms of plague. The disease spread quickly through the inhabitants and led to the deaths of all the villagers. Unattended, the village has now long since crumbled away to nothing, but because of the tragedy of this complete loss of life, perhaps the memory may never entirely fade away.

While the ghost who is said to haunt the land, a White Lady, is not known to have any direct connection to the tragedy, it is not surprisingly considered unlucky to touch any of the stones which lie there.

Much of the land around Llanellan was part of the estate of the family of Lieutenant-Colonel Bowen who fought for Cromwell in the Civil War. His political career, however, took a dramatic turn for the worse when a series of indiscretions led to him losing favour with the strict code of Parliament. This also resulted in him remaining in self-imposed exile in Ireland after the Civil War. His reputation as a womaniser increased at this time, but so did his convinced atheism in a time of religious fervour.

In December 1665, his wife, who had remained in Llanellan with her children, was woken by a great noise which she described as a whirlwind. She also heard the sound of a violent banging on the walls and doors. A voice which sounded like her husband's asked whether he might come to bed with her. She refused and in a state of terror spent the night with other members of the household in prayer.

The disturbances continued for night after night, increasing in intensity as they did so. She reported the terrifying smell of putrefying flesh and sulphur. The people who prayed with her during her nightly vigils felt the physical force of whatever power they were facing. They were beaten so badly by this unseen force that their bodies were bruised until it was too painful for them to continue, and eventually they were forced to leave the house.

Colonel Bowen was called for and although he returned for a short period of time he refused to believe the stories, despite the fact that his wife continued to be as disturbed as before. At last the family moved to Ireland where they hoped to evade whatever ghosts had been tormenting them. The stay was short-lived and Mrs Bowen and some of her children returned to Wales shortly afterwards. Perhaps it is her spirit that now walks the fields of Llanellan.

# LLANFIHANGEL CRUCORNEY

### The One-Legged Ghost

THE Skirrid Inn stands in the shadow of the mountain from which it takes its name (Skirrid-fawr) in the village of Llanfihangel Crucorney. It has often been cited as the oldest inn in Wales and although this may not be completely true it certainly stands on the site of one of the earliest inns, there having been a hostelry here since at least 1170.

The present Skirrid Inn was used as a court by the infamous 'Hanging' Judge Jeffreys after the Monmouth Rebellion in 1685. The resulting executions were also conducted there by hanging those found guilty from a beam above the stairwell.

One of the victims of Judge Jeffreys' harsh sentencing, a one-legged man, succeeded in stabbing himself before his appointment with the noose and died in his cell. His ghost is now said to haunt the inn.

## The Haunted Pool

LLANFIHANGEL CRUCORNEY also has a haunted pool. Here a White Lady, who is believed to be a woman called Eleanor, is said to rise from the waters after dusk wearing a white dress. Her appearance warns of an imminent death in the area.

Eleanor, who appears to have been a little deranged, was the daughter of one of the local Thomas family. Sadly for Eleanor, whatever madness afflicted her was misinterpreted by the locals, who believed that she was a witch. In order to control her powers of witchcraft she was forced by the villagers to wear a hoop of iron around her waist. This contraption led to her receiving the name of the Lady of the Ring and no doubt it was this weight which led to her watery death.

## A White Lady and a Green Man

LLANFIHANGEL COURT is an impressive mansion built and extended between the 14th and the 16th century. It is said to be haunted by two spirits, one a White Lady and the other a small, green man with piercing green eyes. The Green Man appears in the White Room, and while there is no evidence as to who he might be, it is possible that he is the ghost of one of the servants who wore a green uniform.

The stairway bears marks which have been there for many years, and legend has it that these are bloodstains from a fatal sword fight which took place a long time ago. Perhaps it is this incident which connects the Green Man to the house.

The White Lady is said to make her entrance in the hallway on the stroke of midnight. On the occasions that she appears she progresses through the house and then outside onto the terrace. There she pauses for a moment and lets out a terrifying scream before she heads along a fir-tree-lined avenue to a wooded area nearby, where she disappears. A testament to the story is that the wooded area has become known as Lady Wood.

Although the identity of the ghost is not known, a grisly discovery made some time ago may offer a possible explanation for her presence in the house.

Several years ago, the terrace where the White Lady pauses was lifted in the course of some work being carried out. At the very spot where the spirit lets out her scream a shallow grave was found beneath the flagstones. When this was excavated a skeleton was discovered with a bullet still lodged in it. Perhaps the White Lady was the murder victim and is now re-enacting the moments leading up to her death.

# LLANGYNWYD

### A Vengeful Spirit

THE village of Llangynwyd stands to the south of Maesteg, close to where the counties of West and Mid Glamorgan meet. Two stories persist in the village and it may not be unreasonable to suspect that they could in some way be connected. They may even relate to the same ghost.

One winter in the late 18th century an old beggar by the name of Philip Thomas was granted permission by the owner of Pentre Farm to sleep in one of the outhouses. From the time of his arrival, Catherine, one of the maids at the farm, took exception to him. Her taunts and torments were intended to drive poor Philip away but they failed to have any effect. Frustrated by her lack of success, Catherine took to more devious methods. She complained to her employer that Philip was the one who was pestering her. This course of action also failed and Philip was still allowed to stay on.

Shortly after this, Catherine found the old man collapsed on the floor of the outhouse near to death. He begged her for a drink of water, but in keeping with her previous treatment of him she refused his request. While she stood watching, the old man died.

It is quite possible that Catherine may have come to regret her lack of charity but it appears that Thomas's ghost was in search of revenge. From the moment of Philip's death, Catherine complained of something snatching at her clothes, and this developed into unseen hands pushing and slapping her. On one occasion the vengeful spirit is even said to have thrown a bucket of water over her.

This vengeance grew more dangerous and less specific in its aim and when the old man's ghost began to throw stones around the farmhouse, steps were taken to bring the matter to a halt.

The farmer brought in the Reverend Parry, the local vicar, to conduct an exorcism, but without success. When the vicar was told by onlookers that the ghost was behind him, he fled from the farm in terror. The farmer then called on the services of the Reverend Jones from the parish of Glynogwr who had more experience in such matters. The rite of exorcism was conducted and the ghost of the man who had been afforded hospitality in life was driven out of the farm.

The second story dates from a little after these events and concerns a house said to harbour a strange presence – a number of people complaining both of an eerie coldness and a feeling of being watched.

The house in question was the old vicarage, once the home of the unfortunate Reverend Parry.


# LLANTWIT MAJOR

### The Black Lady of Boverton

THE remains of Boverton Castle stand on ground on the outskirts of Llantwit Major. The town itself is one of the oldest in Wales, and the site of the castle has been used over the years as a stronghold for successive invasion forces.

During the reign of Richard I, the castle was the property of the Earl of Gloucester. The Earl was the father of Hadwisa who became the first wife of the king's infamous brother, Prince John. When John ascended to the throne he divorced Hadwisa in order to marry Isabella of Angouleme. After the divorce, Hadwisa spent the rest of her life at Boverton Castle, almost as an outcast from society. The story goes that despite his treatment of her, Hadwisa never stopped loving John.

The castle was dismantled in the early part of the 19th century and, during the work, the ghostly figure of a woman dressed completely in black and with long black hair was seen on several occasions. The workmen also claimed that they heard her weeping.

Locals decided that this was the ghost of Hadwisa, wearing her widow's weeds, still mourning her husband hundreds of years after her own death. She has long been known as the Black Lady of Boverton.

## An Avaricious Daughter-in-Law

IN the village of Llantwit Major itself, there once lived a tailor and his wife Barbara. When the tailor's mother lay on her deathbed, she entrusted Barbara with the duty of dividing her money between the family when her estate had been settled. Instead, when the mother died, Barbara kept the money for herself. It was not long before the spirit of the old lady began to exact her revenge on her treacherous daughter-in-law.

Night after night, the ghost would pinch Barbara until she was black and blue, relentlessly denying her sleep. Eventually Barbara fell ill through lack of rest and it was then that the ghost appeared to her, giving her the choice of completing the deathbed wish, or of throwing the money downstream into the nearby river Ogmore.

Selfishly, Barbara chose the second option rather than risk the shame of confessing her deception to the rest of the family. As soon as she had made this decision, the ghost swept Barbara high above the town until she reached the river. Once there she was given the signal to throw the money, but as she did so she aimed it upstream rather than down as the ghost had instructed. The ghost's anger grew and after being buffeted by the wind Barbara was dropped into a whirlpool.

Late in the evening, bellringers at the local church discovered Barbara lying bruised and battered on the river bank. She was unable to explain how she had come to be there, but from then on the whole of her family, including her husband who had in no way been involved in his wife's deceit, were plagued by strange noises in the house. Even after her death, other villagers claimed that her children remained ghost-ridden.

# LLANVITHYN

## Walled Up in the Monastery

NORTH of the village of Llancarfan is an area known as Llanvithyn which was once the site of a monastery.

At some time in the past, when the monastery was still standing, a man who was attempting to escape from his enemies sought sanctuary with the monks. He was admitted but their protection was not enough. He was recaptured, had his leg hacked off and was then walled up in the monastery. His body lay there until several centuries later when it was discovered while alterations to the building were being carried out.

It should also be borne in mind that 'walling up' was a punishment sometimes meted out by the monks against someone who had transgressed against them.

Surprisingly enough, it is not the ghost of this poor unfortunate who haunts the grounds but that of his wife, still looking for her husband.

# MARGAM

## The Ghosts of Margam Castle

STANDING on the eastern side of the town of Port Talbot, Margam Castle and the grounds which make up the park are now one of the most popular tourist attractions in South Wales. From time to time the number of visitors is boosted by the arrival of scores of ghost hunters.

The grounds of Margam Park contain the remains of a 12th-century Cistercian priory which itself boasts a famous orangery. Originally laid out during the reign of Queen Mary, the orangery was planted after the fortuitous arrival of a consignment of orange trees rescued from a Spanish ship which was wrecked off the coast nearby. The ruins of the priory are said to be haunted, not surprisingly, by the ghostly figure of a monk in a white habit.

Local legend has it that this spirit may be the ghost of Twm Gelwydd Teg (Tom of the Fair Lies). Twm was a monk who was well known in the area at the time and used to work at the grange belonging to the priory. It was said that he had an almost magical ability to tell the future, but always he expressed whatever he saw in strange ways.

Twm would tend to predict good fortune for those who had been kind to him, and less pleasant futures for those who had wronged him. Sadly his predictions for good fortune rarely came true, but the unpleasant ones always did. Whether this was a case of blinkered vision or an ability to curse is impossible to say.

Sir George Herbert of Cynfig Castle once had Twm thrown into jail, leaving the poor monk feeling very angry. Shortly after his release a feast was held to celebrate the birth of a son and heir to Sir George. While there was a great deal of rejoicing over the matter, when Twm heard of the celebrations he said, 'What a fuss about a baby which will be hanged by the string of his forehead-band.'

The news of Twm's declaration was relayed to Sir George, who, although not believing in Twm's prescience, did everything in his power to ensure his son's safety. The child was placed in the charge of a nurse with strict instructions that the infant should be watched closely day and night.

The baby was quite contented and in good health, but after a little while someone told Sir George and his wife that the nurse was suffering with an infectious skin complaint. The nurse was sent for at once, but when she arrived they found that her skin was as healthy as their own. When they all returned to the nursery, however, the baby was dead in its cradle. The forehead-band had slipped down while it had been left alone, and the child had twisted his hands inside it so that it had tightened around his neck, causing the helpless infant to choke to death.

This story has echoes of the tale of Sleeping Beauty, although with a less happy ending, and is perhaps a good illustration of how the folk tales of one country can become adapted and reshaped into the culture of another.

On another occasion Twm was confronted one day by a young man who had tormented and ridiculed the monk many times. The young man, who was about to set off on a bird watching expedition, stopped the monk and asked, 'What lies do you have for me today, Twm?'

Twm, who took the man's jibes without complaint, replied without hesitating, 'You will die three deaths before nightfall.'

The young man laughed at the monk and his strange ways and walked away. He dismissed Twm's statement, thinking how on earth could anyone die three times in a single day? Sadly for him, the prophecy was fulfilled.

The young man's day was made quite early on in his expedition when he found a kite's nest at the top of a tall tree which overhung a river. Although the climb was precarious, he succeeded in reaching the top. As he put his hand in the nest to check for eggs he was bitten by an adder that the mother bird had caught as food for her chicks which had already hatched. The shock of the snake's venomous bite caused the man to lose his balance in fright. As he fell from the tree he caught his head on a sturdy branch and broke his neck. He then landed in the river and subsequently drowned. Snake bite, broken neck and drowning. Three certain deaths.

A very similar ghost to that of Tom of the Fair Lies is said to appear at a nearby property which once belonged to Neath Abbey. When this particular ghostly monk is sighted his appearance is often accompanied by the sound of religious chanting.

The grounds of Margam Park itself are dominated by the much restored castle. This spectacular Gothic mansion was completed for Christopher Rice Mansel Talbot, whose family gave Port Talbot its name and helped create much of the wealth which established the town as an industrial base.

The house has long been said to be home to at least two ghosts. One of these is a White Lady, while the other spirit is that of a male figure in Victorian dress. It is the White Lady who makes the most frequent appearances in the house, but recent work at the castle appears to have released a much more malevolent spirit.

During 1995 Margam Castle went through a major period of restoration. This involved disturbing a number of rooms which had previously lain untouched for over a hundred years. The result of this has been a fairly significant increase in the number of sightings and strange experiences. Prior to these renovations, it had been considered almost commonplace amongst the workers at the park to catch a glimpse from the corner of an eye of the White Lady of Margam, and they seemed to take her in their stride. This latest wave of visitations has been more disturbing and the spirits much more aggressive.

Over a period of no more than a few days in October 1995 there appeared to be what, by previous standards, could have been described as a frenzy of activity. One visitor swore that she had seen the legendary White Lady of Margam, while one of the workers in the Orangery told his bosses that he had felt a strange presence and that he had also heard a mysterious hissing sound.

On the Saturday afternoon came the culmination of these disturbances. Two kitchen workers, Claire Francis and Annette Webley, were terrified by the sight of an eight foot tall, shadowy figure which also hissed at them in the same way that the other worker had reported. The sight and sound of this apparition caused them to flee in terror. They have both since refused to enter the kitchens again alone.

The castle has traditionally hosted a Hallowe'en party for many years. In 1995 however, after the publicity surrounding these events, in excess of 500 tickets were sold. The staff were so inundated with requests for tickets that they were forced to arrange a second event for the day before Hallowe'en in order to cope with the high level of demand.

# MERTHYR TYDFIL

### The Black Pool

NEAR the industrial town of Merthyr Tydfil lies a stretch of water known as the Black Pool. The area around the lake is said to be haunted by the ghost of a beautiful woman who wears long, white, flowing clothes. The ghost seems to have much in common with tales of sirens and of the Lorelei as she tries to attract unsuspecting victims to the pool with the intention of luring them to a watery death.

# MONMOUTH

### The Haunting of Lower Bailey Pit

CLOSE to the market town of Monmouth are areas known as the Bailey Pits which were once the sites of medieval settlements. Old Bailey Pit has long since been reclaimed by woodland and little now remains. A few broken walls are all there is to serve as reminder of the ancient farmhouse which had once stood there. Upper Bailey Pit too has almost disappeared into Monmouth Forest, all that is except the old track along which a ghostly coach and horses has been seen to travel. Lower Bailey Pit on the other hand has stood much longer, and in the 1960s had the reputation of being one of the most haunted houses in Monmouth.

At that time the house was purported to be the home of at least two ghosts. The first, although never seen, was that of a man with a wooden leg. His footsteps in an upstairs room could often be heard in the room below. Loud screams were also said to have been heard coming from the cellar. These spectral cries have been attributed to the ghost of a maid who was murdered on her way down the cellar stairs.

According to Stephen Clarke in his booklet *The most haunted house in Monmouth* (Monmouth Archaeological Society, 1975), the house was empty by the late 1960s and had fallen into disrepair. At this time the most detailed account of the haunting was recorded.

One hot summer's day a plumber was carrying out work on the property and was about to disconnect the water supply to one of the outhouses. While working he heard a door slam shut and he went to investigate. He searched the house and found it, as he expected it to be, empty. In the absence of any breeze he could find no explanation for the door having slammed. He pushed the door open, it was one which led into one of the downstairs rooms, and made to leave. As he turned his back on the door it slammed shut again. This time he decided to look no further and left the house feeling more than a little uneasy.

Some time later he returned to the house with a friend who was interested in the paranormal, and Stephen Clarke. The three of them sat in silence in the downstairs room in question and waited. It was not long before their vigil proved fruitful. They heard footsteps, then a strange tapping noise and a loud thud coming from somewhere else in the house. The friend with the interest in the paranormal declared that he felt a 'presence' in the building and, fearing that it might be evil, implored the others to leave the house with him. They did so, much to the disappointment of Stephen Clarke.

In 1970 Clarke heard from an archaeologist about a group of six friends who, knowing of Lower Bailey Pit's reputation, went into the house one rainy night with the intention of holding a seance. Almost as soon as they entered they felt they were falling under the influence of the house. They gathered together in the same room as the previous trio and found that it began to grow cold quickly. On hearing strange noises, including footsteps, coming from an upstairs room they all became unsettled. One of the three men, John, became so worried that he made everyone leave and all six of them fled back onto the driveway. David, the brother of the frightened man, shone a torch at the window of the bedrooms from where the footsteps had emanated. He insisted that there must be someone still inside the house. While the others tried their best to dissuade him he ran back into the house to investigate.

When the others began to follow him back into the house he called back to them, 'It's my father.' He then began to run up the stairs, leaving some of the others standing at the bottom, stunned by this statement.

By this time John had re-entered the house and, despite his obvious fear, started as if to follow his brother up the stairs. David shouted again, this time in a more concerned voice, 'It's coming after me.'

The others shone their torches up the stairs to reveal, to their horror, that the tread behind him was bowing and groaning under some invisible weight. These ghostly footsteps were also disturbing the dust which lay on the stairs. Throughout this, the sound of heavy footfalls echoed around the walls.

Once the sounds had died away, all five of them cautiously carried on up the stairs in search of David who had failed to return. They found him in a state of hysteria in one of the bedrooms, and as they tried to calm him while at the same time encouraging him to leave, the sense of all-pervading evil descended on them. None of them had the courage to try to leave the room. Together, at John's suggestion, they sang to ward off the evil and to keep their spirits up. They sang 'Bread of Heaven' until the presence faded away and they were at last able to leave the house.

Disregarding their experience, David tried to return to the house again, convinced that he had seen his father. This was despite the fact that his father had died when he was a baby and he had never known him.

In the summer of 1993, Lower Bailey Pit was destroyed by fire. Although it has since been rebuilt there have been no further unusual incidents reported.

# MOUNTAIN ASH

### Guto Nyth Bran, the ghostly runner

A gravestone in the churchyard at St Gwynno's in Mountain Ash marks the final resting place of the body, if not the spirit, of a most remarkable athlete. Inscribed in the stone are the words 'Twelve miles in seven minutes under the hour', a noteworthy feat even by today's standards especially when considering the terrain over which this was achieved.

Guto Nyth Bran was born in 1700 on the remote hill farm from which he took his name. Nyth Bran means a crow or raven's nest. Guto made a reputation for himself by taking on all comers in races over the local hills. More than one of his neighbours made easy money by betting on him to win.

In 1737, Guto raced against an equally renowned English runner. The race was hard and he was pushed more severely than he had ever been before but the fear of losing to an Englishman spurred him on to victory. Sadly the race took too much out of him and Guto collapsed with exhaustion, dying shortly after crossing the finish line. His headstone is also inscribed with a heart, which may reflect the affection with which he was held by those who knew and admired him, or simply the fact that his heart had finally failed him.

The sight of a ghostly runner, charging across the hills at midnight, has been reported many times through the years. Perhaps this is Guto, continuing to run his races.

# MUMBLES

### A Back Seat Driver

THE road from Swansea to Mumbles is a fast dual carriageway which is in almost constant use, even well into the early hours of the morning. As the road approaches Mumbles itself it reduces to a single carriageway and is little wider than it was in years gone by, despite the flow of traffic.

A colleague of mine used to drive to Mumbles on this road every morning at around 8.30 and return shortly after 5 pm. Fortunately for him, this was contrary to the major flow of traffic as more people live in Mumbles and work in Swansea than the other way around. Anyone who has driven on the same road every day for any length of time will recognise the situation that my colleague found himself in. On many mornings he would be driving, almost on automatic pilot as the turns in the road had become second nature, only to realise a few minutes later that he could not remember having driven along a certain stretch of the road.

One morning when he was in this state he had a sudden urge to slow down, despite the fact that he was doing no more than the speed limit. When he took the next bend he saw that there had been an accident. He also claimed that he had a strange feeling that there was someone sitting on the back seat. This happened to him not once, but three times over a period of months, and each time he felt that he had a passenger looking over his shoulder.

It would be easy to dismiss this story but I filed it away at the back of my mind until a few years later when someone else told me that they had experienced the same thing. Is this some kind of ghostly back seat driver?

## A Troubled Spirit at Oystermouth Castle

ON what is now Newton Road in the seaside town of Mumbles stand the well preserved remains of Oystermouth Castle. The castle dates back to the 13th century and while the age and history of a building like this would normally lead to a legacy of ghost stories this is not the case in this instance. There is, however, a single story which refuses to die away, thanks to irregular sightings of one particularly troubled spirit.

The ghost is that of a young woman who has been noticed outside the castle walls on several occasions. Whenever seen she has been crying and the back of her white dress has been torn away to reveal the bloody weals which are no doubt the cause of her anguish.

It is easy to believe that the woman may have been flogged to death on the whipping posts which still stand in the castle dungeons today. But who she was and why she should have died in such a manner remains a mystery.

## Disturbing Sightings at Oystermouth Cemetery

LESS than a mile from the castle is one of the eeriest places I have ever visited, Oystermouth Cemetery. In October 1995, along with fellow horror writer Mike O'Driscoll, I had been invited to record a short piece on Hallowe'en and horror fiction in general. The filming was due to take place in the late afternoon, but owing to problems experienced by the television crew we were kept waiting in the cold cemetery as the sun went down.

As twilight approached a low-hanging mist developed, and while the grounds were not entirely deserted it began to feel a very lonely place. The most disturbing aspect was that people who were walking or cycling along the long, straight paths which rose and fell into the distance would appear and disappear without warning.

While I do not know of any ghostly sightings within the cemetery I would not be surprised if people had misinterpreted this weird phenomenon. The place is not to be recommended to those of a vivid imagination or a nervous disposition.

## The Ghost Went Shopping Too

AT one end of Titchbourne Street in Mumbles, stands a house that was once the blacksmith's forge. The building is around 300 years old and, like several others in the area, some of its walls are almost a metre thick. It appears to be haunted by the spirit of the blacksmith.

The house is currently owned by the Reverend Borthwick, a hospital chaplain, and although neither the Reverend or his family have actually seen the ghost they have sensed its presence many times. They say that although it has remained unseen, it has a distinctly masculine aura, and while not unfriendly, it is a little mischievous.

The Reverend Borthwick bought the property in the mid 1980s and first heard of the ghost when he was speaking to his new neighbours shortly afterwards. The neighbours were somewhat surprised that the previous owner had not informed him of the strange occurrences which had taken place. To be honest, I would have been surprised if he had! Including a ghost along with the fixtures and fittings is unlikely to be the sort of thing which increases either value or marketability.

Not long after moving into the house, the Reverend Borthwick began to discover some of the manifestations for himself. Windows were thrown open, even when winter arrived, almost as if the ghost was still experiencing the heat of the forge. It was also not uncommon for lights to be switched on and off. On one occasion Mrs Borthwick placed a vase on a linen cloth only to discover a few minutes later that it had been turned upside down. The cloth which it had been standing on had been pushed inside.

The ghost also seems to attach itself to the owners of the house rather than just the building or its grounds, as the Reverend and his wife discovered one day when they visited a DIY store in Swansea in search of a timer for their central heating system. It appeared that the ghost had decided to come shopping with them. As they were examining the range of products on display, they were astonished to see them start to fall to the ground. An attendant came rushing over to see what the commotion was, but was unable to discover the cause of the disruption.

Their daughter, then a student at the University of Swansea, reported hearing footsteps in the house. When one of her friends stayed overnight the friend woke, after dreaming that cold water was being poured over her. On collecting her thoughts she realised that the bed was soaked with water.

On another occasion some of the daughter's friends came to the house to watch a rugby match on television. The friends had all heard of the ghost that was claimed to share the house, and in good fun one of them suggested that it should turn the television on for them. It duly obliged.

The Reverend Borthwick says that the ghost has rarely failed to demonstrate its presence when asked to do so, as if performing party tricks. Apart from lights having been switched on and off, and windows opened almost on command, it has never seemed to pose any sort of threat.

The Reverend says that he now feels quite at home with the ghost and sees no need to exorcise it.

# NANTYGLO

## The Horseman Returns to Hafod-y-Ddol

HAFOD-Y-DDOL was built towards the end of the 18th century in the town of Nantyglo as a private house, probably for a wealthy owner of one of the ironworks in the area which along with coal mining provided substantial levels of employment. The property, like so many other large houses, was not long in acquiring a ghost of its own.

Within a few years of the house having been built, it was owned by Richard Rowland, who is said to have trained a winner of the Derby at Nantyglo and was well known within the equine fraternity. One cold night he was returning from Abergavenny where he had been attending a Hunt Ball. Unfortunately he was more than a little the worse for drink and was not really in a fit state to ride his horse. On the journey home the horse was probably startled by something, as it certainly threw Richard from its back and left him lying injured on the mountainside. There he lay, undiscovered and bleeding, and sometime during the night he died.

The horse continued its journey riderless, and arrived at Hafod-y-Ddol sometime after midnight. Its iron shod hooves clattered on the cobbles of the courtyard, rousing the servants. When it was discovered that the horse had returned home without its master they knew that an accident must have occurred. A search party was organised but it was daybreak before they found the body of Richard Rowland where he had fallen – but by then it was too late.

Subsequent owners of the house have been woken in the night by the sound of hooves on cobbles but when they have looked out onto the courtyard they have found there to be no one there. While they accept that it may have been that these sounds were a fragment of a dream they have not been able to explain those which followed. As they lay awake in their beds they heard the sound of jangling spurs and the step of heavy boots on the landing leading to Richard's old room. The sounds often continued for several days but nothing was ever seen.

In 1924 the house was turned into Nantyglo Grammar School, but by then the legend was well known in the area. Groups of school children would hide themselves in the building until after the property had been locked up for the night in an attempt to see or hear the ghostly rider of Hafod-y-Ddol. Although the children were disappointed that their vigils proved fruitless, many people who have lived nearby are sure that they have heard the sound of hooves clattering across the playground.

# NEATH

### The Ghostly Cockle-Seller in Victoria Gardens

DURING the early part of the 19th century a distinctive group of Neath women were known throughout the county of Glamorgan and could be identified quite easily by their thickset build and patterned clothes. They made their living by travelling around the county selling cockles, for which much of the coastline around Swansea is famous. They also sold needles, pins and various other odds and ends. These gypsies were known as the Merched y Mera (women of the Mera) and lived in a matriarchal system where the woman was all powerful and the children took their surname from their mother's family name rather than their father's.

There have been many sightings of one of these women, now in ghostly form, in Victoria Gardens in Neath. One observer reported that she had been sitting in the gardens watching the children play when she saw a large woman standing very close to her who had not been there an instant before. The woman was carrying two large baskets and wore old-fashioned clothes.

Several people walked past the strange woman without seeming to notice her, but as they passed she held out her baskets for them to examine. In sympathy, the woman who was sitting on the bench reached into her purse for some change to give to the gypsy. When she looked up, the woman and her wares had disappeared and she felt quite strange as she sat with the coins still in her hand.

In almost all of the accounts of the ghostly woman she has been seen trying unsuccessfully to sell the contents of her baskets, and she disappears after several fruitless attempts to find buyers.


## The White Lady of Gnoll House

ALSO in the town of Neath stands an area of parkland which has for some time been known as Gnoll Gardens, or simply the Gnoll. The park covers a large stretch of the hillside above the rugby ground which bears the same name. Within the park are the ruins of Gnoll House which are now little more than low walls marking out the rooms of the ground floor. Once, however, it was a splendid property.

The house was purchased by Henry Grant in around 1810, but sadly he met with an early death. Several people have reported seeing a White Lady in the grounds, particularly in the area close to where the house once stood, and she is heard to be calling, 'Henry, Henry'.

There can be little doubt that this spirit is that of Lady Grant, still mourning the loss of her husband.

## Pounding at the Door

NEATH ABBEY was built in the 12th century by the Cistercian order which had a strong presence in this particular part of South Wales. The abbey now stands in ruins and yet is still a peaceful place, at least during the day. Sometimes at night, however, people living in the area nearby have heard the strange sound of banging coming from the ruins.

When Edward II's position came under threat from powerful friends of his wife who led a revolt against him, he escaped to Neath. Edward had often given money to the monks, particularly in connection with providing funds for the building of monasteries. The Cistercians were therefore only too pleased to offer sanctuary when he needed it. But while he was staying at the abbey, one of the monks betrayed his presence to his enemies. As a direct result of this the King was captured and taken to Berkeley Castle. There he was tried and executed within a very short space of time.

The monks of Neath Abbey, on realising that they had failed in their duty to provide sanctuary and maintain the confidence of any who stayed with them, expelled the treacherous monk responsible.

Local legend has it that the banging that can be heard at night is the dishonoured monk still pounding at the front door of the abbey, begging for re-admittance. An alternative suggestion is that perhaps it is the ghost of Edward II himself who has returned, seeking refuge – or perhaps revenge.

## Sobbing on the Banks of the River Neath

MANY years ago a Methodist school teacher from Aberdulais in the Vale of Neath fell in love with a man who regularly came to Neath on business. Her mother warned her not to become involved with the man but she took no notice. Instead she continued to lavish both money and gifts on him. In time the man promised to marry her, but not while her mother was still alive.

Eventually the mother died, but far from fulfilling his promise the man stopped seeing the teacher altogether. Devastated by the loss of both her lover and her mother, she left a note in the coal bucket and went down to the river. There she threw herself in the fast running water and drowned.

Her ghost remains in the area and the sound of her sobbing has been heard on the river bank.

# NEWPORT

## St Gwynlliw and the Pirates

IN the early part of the 5th century, in the town of Newport, there lived a man of about 30 who had the reputation of being the biggest drunkard in the town. As he was also a wealthy man there was little to prevent his excesses.

His wife by comparison was a religious woman and prayed with her children that her husband might give up this way of life and become a Christian. Her prayers were answered one night when the man heard a voice saying to him, 'Forsake your evil ways and turn to me.'

From that moment, like St Paul on the way to Damascus, he became a changed man and devoted the rest of his life to the service of God and his money to feeding the poor. His life became so holy that he was given the name St Gwynlliw.

As a sign of his love of God St Gwynlliw decided to build a church but his dilemma was where to site it. One night in his sleep while he was troubled with this problem, he was visited by an angel who told him to look for an ox which was pure white except for a black spot on its forehead. The next day, St Gwynlliw began his search for the ox and found one which fitted the description at the top of Stow Hill. Straight away he began to make arrangements for the building of his church on that very spot.

In the final year of the century the church was completed and he named it St Woolos', but shortly after that St Gwynlliw died. Before he did so he placed a curse on anyone who should desecrate the church or steal from it.

In the year following St Gwynlliw's death, pirates sailed up the river Usk to the stretch of water where the Alexandra Docks were built hundreds of years later. As they approached Newport they could see the church standing high on the hill and they decided that a building of such stature must contain magnificent treasures. Under cover of darkness the pirates made their way into the town and up the hill to the church. The sight that met them on entering it must have exceeded even their wildest expectations. There they found a huge golden cross encrusted with precious stones, along with an array of jewelled chalices and other church vessels.

Undetected, they returned to their ship with the booty and set sail quickly. The waters were calm at first, but as they left the mouth of the river and went out into the Bristol Channel the weather began to change quickly. A storm swept black clouds in from nowhere, obscuring the moon which had lit their way, and the sea became more violent. Riding on the wind came the spirit of *St Gwynlliw* with his arms outstretched, seeking to fulfil his own curse. He swooped down onto the ship and gathered up the treasures from the terrified pirates to return them to his church. As he left, the ship was caught in the grip of the storm, sending it to the bottom of the Channel to the sound of the pirates' screams. The next morning the bodies of the drowned sailors were found floating back up the river in witness of the devastation.

The church has undergone restoration and renovation over the centuries but it has remained virtually undefiled since the time of the pirates' sacrilege. This may be due to the protection afforded by the ghost of St Gwynlliw, or perhaps through fear of the curse.

The only other damage done to the church was carried out by the hand, or rather the gun, of one of Oliver Cromwell's troops. The headless statue which resulted can still be seen in a nook of one of the towers.


### Summerland

FRANCES POWLES is a medium, a clairvoyant and also a clairaudient, but more than any of these she acts as a guide. With the aid of a group of spirits she refers to as 'The Committee', she guides lost and troubled spirits from this world to the place she calls Summerland. This is the story of just one family Frances has helped by leading the ghosts who were disturbing them to a better place.

Vincent and Lisa Derek, along with their young son Luke, had by December 1995 been living in a modern terraced house in Newport for two years. Shortly before Christmas of that year the family were sitting in the living room when they heard voices coming from upstairs. Naturally, at first they thought there were intruders in the house. On investigation they found they were not of the kind they were expecting.

Vincent went upstairs to challenge whoever it was that had entered their home, but after searching the bedrooms one by one found no one there. When he stepped back out onto the landing, somewhat puzzled after checking the final bedroom, he was confronted for a moment by the ghost of a young boy of around ten years old. The boy was waving his arms but was not threatening in any way. Vincent felt that it was more likely that he was looking for someone to play with.

Over the next few days the voices became more regular, lights flickered without warning and the temperature of the house would drop suddenly. On Boxing Day this came to a head when the noises started again. Vincent went up the stairs to investigate, but as he neared the top a gust of wind blew through the house. The lights flickered and flashed on and off and the smoke alarms were triggered. The family fled the house in terror and sought refuge with relatives.

Although the Dereks were not Catholics they contacted Father Michael Hare of St Patrick's church. Father Michael was unable to offer much in the way of practical help, feeling that the family would need the strength of faith to expel whatever spirits had taken residence in their house, but they were not of his flock. He did, however, acknowledge that their worries were genuine and he said prayers, sprinkled holy water and blessed the house. Despite this the manifestations continued. It was then that Vincent and Lisa were put in touch with Frances Powles, who subsequently visited their house.

As soon as she went upstairs she sensed a presence in the bedroom that the family used as a storeroom.

There she found the same cold spot she had experienced in many previous encounters with spirits. When Vincent came upstairs with cups of tea she was already in conversation with the spirits of both the young boy and an old man. She described the man to Vincent, but he did not recognise him. Frances understood that the man was confused about what he was to do now that he was dead and it seemed that the boy was trying to help him.

Frances then called on one of 'The Committee' to help lead the man and the boy to Summerland. When this third spirit tried to lead the old man away he became very agitated and kept saying something about the electricity. He would not agree to pass on until Frances promised to warn the family, which she gladly undertook to do. She then saw Summerland appear on the wall of the bedroom and the three spirits stepped through.

As she had promised, Frances told Vincent about the warning, and as soon as she had finished Vincent knew that the ghost had been his own father. He told Frances that in later years his father had become obsessed with electrical safety, sometimes getting up in the middle of the night to check switches.

The warning was not totally unfounded as it was subsequently discovered that the smoke detectors which had been triggered during the manifestations were wired into the mains incorrectly.

When Father Hare called at the house some time later he declared that something had gone from the house. Although he remains firm in his own faith, he acknowledges that some people, like Frances, have gifts which can prove useful. A few days after this, Father Hare received a telephone call from another family of non-Catholics who were also hearing voices and seeing apparitions. Frances was called upon again and two more spirits were led successfully to Summerland.

# PENNARD

## The Castle's Tales

AT Pennard on the Gower peninsula stand the remains of a Norman castle. The castle is in a far worse state of preservation than the one at Oystermouth, leaving its original appearance very much to the imagination.

The castle was in fact abandoned within a couple of hundred years of its completion, a fairly short lifespan for a structure designed to withstand the rigours of attack and last indefinitely. Even before it was fully occupied, drifting sands had begun to encroach on the land and it was this which eventually rendered the castle uninhabitable.

A local folk tale relates, however, that it was a band of fairies who had been attacked by the Norman lord while they danced outside the castle walls that had caused the destruction of the castle. In order to force the Normans from their land the fairies raised a fierce sandstorm in retaliation and destroyed the building, causing the Normans to flee.

There is also said to be a fearsome Gwrach y Rhibyn who stalks the lands around the castle. It guards treasure supposedly buried in the sand dunes close to the castle ruins. The legend goes on to say that anyone who dares to sleep within the castle walls between sunset and sunrise runs the risk of being cursed by the Gwrach y Rhibyn and incurring her wrath.

A young man once spent a night there in response to a bet that he would be afraid to see the night through in such a place. Perhaps he discovered the secret dangers of the castle. He was certainly left in such a state that he was never able to speak of it. On the following morning he was found lying unconscious on one of the sand dunes. The whole of his body was covered in bruises and his face was smeared with dried blood from a number of deep scratches. Worse still, his mind had become deranged through his experience and he never recovered sufficiently to be able to tell the true nature of his ordeal.

Locals were of course convinced of his fate. They had no doubt that he had been visited by the Gwrach y Rhibyn.

# PORTHCAWL

### The Sound of Footsteps on the Path

IN a house in 18th-century Porthcawl, a married couple were woken in the night by the sound of footsteps coming towards them, as if several people were walking up the path. The husband looked out of the bedroom window and was disturbed to find that there was no one there. He returned to bed and he and his wife sat holding hands without speaking as the noise continued.

The sounds outside stopped and there seemed to be people in the kitchen. There was then the loud thump of something being dropped onto the kitchen table and the house went quiet.

The couple stayed in bed, although unable to sleep, until it was light when they crept downstairs, afraid of what they might find. There was nothing strange in the kitchen, nor in any other part of the house and nothing had been disturbed. The husband went to work as normal and when he returned that evening his wife had nothing new to report. Although they still felt uneasy about what they had heard, the house remained quiet for the next few days and their minds became easier. Then there came a knock on the door.

It was a man who had come to tell them that their only son had drowned three days earlier, probably the night they had heard the strange noises. His body was brought to them, carried on a plank and wrapped in a blanket. The men who bore the corpse wore heavy boots and their footsteps rang along the path, sending what the couple thought to be a final shiver down their spines. Then came the bump as the plank, and the body, were dropped onto the kitchen table.

## The Maid of Sker

ONCE standing in splendid isolation on the stretch of coastline between Nottage and Sker Point, Sker House was the inspiration for R. D. Blackmore (the author of *Lorna Doone*) to write his novel *The Maid of Sker*. The property was originally built in 1554 by Christopher Tuberville, and the house remained the family home for his descendants for several generations. Sadly, owing to many years of neglect, the house has lain derelict since 1969.

The best known ghost story told about the house concerns Elizabeth William (The Maid of Sker). Elizabeth is supposed to have been imprisoned by her father in an upstairs room in order to prevent her from seeing her lover. She was held captive and in chains until her death, and even now is still unable to leave the house. Her ghost is said to appear in that same room, accompanied by the sound of the clanking of the chains that her father had used to restrain her.

Other tales of the house and the immediate area abound. A ghostly white horse has been reported from time to time and it is said that if it appears on the night of the full moon it is a portent of impending death to anyone who should see it.

A strange white light has also been seen hovering above Sker and Tusker Rocks, along with a ghostly white ship just out to sea. Perhaps this is some sort of phantom re-enactment of the activities of the gang of wreckers whose activities were once notorious in the Southerndown area.

# PORT TALBOT

## The Morfa Colliery Disaster

ALTHOUGH there are no longer any outward signs remaining of Morfa Colliery, its pithead used to stand at Taibach on the edge of what is now Port Talbot. Not only was it the site of one of the worst mining disasters in South Wales during the 19th or possibly any other century, but the impending doom was also foretold by a number of omens.

On Sunday, 9th March 1890 a great white bird was seen resting on the winding gear that stood sentry over the mine. The bird watched and waited, and its presence was seen as an omen of impending disaster.

This was not to be the first accident the mine had witnessed, nor the first time that such signs or portents had been seen. None of the previous signs, however, had predicted anything as severe as what followed shortly afterwards.

In the days and weeks that led up to the tragedy there had been the sounds of roof falls that echoed all around the mine workings when no such cave-ins had taken place. An apparition was seen in the cage while it was taking miners down the shaft, and another jumped onto the underground train. Although not recognised immediately, this latter ghost was later identified by some of the other men on the train as a miner who had died in the colliery some years earlier. Others claimed to have heard the voices of colleagues who had died in previous accidents, screaming and pleading for help.

Perhaps most dramatically of all, as the day of the disaster approached, hundreds of rats were seen scuttling from the mine before the start of the night shift as if deserting a sinking ship, although it is not recorded quite how they achieved this feat. . . That night, corpse candles (Canwyll Corff), flickering blue lights that are associated with impending death, were seen within the mine workings. A certain sign of death to come.

This final sign proved too much for many of the miners, and heeding the warnings they did not enter the mine on that fateful morning. Even those who were not of a superstitious nature took notice, naturally enough being more than a little afraid of naked flames underground.

None of these forebodings so much as hinted at the terrible misery that would be brought upon almost every family in the town by the dreadful underground explosion which followed. By the time the rescue attempt had ended, the tally of dead miners had reached 87. There was probably no one in the town who did not have a relative or friend injured or killed in the devastation.

# REYNOLDSTON

## The Lady in the Chair

IN June 1960, a couple were staying with relatives in the village of Reynoldston. They had visited the house many times before, but on this occasion the husband had the strange feeling that there was a woman sitting in an empty chair at mealtimes. While there was no visual apparition he had a mental impression so strong that on several occasions he looked up to speak to her as if she was there.

Although the husband was sceptical about the existence of ghosts, his wife was a firm believer in the afterlife, and she readily accepted that what he was experiencing was a ghostly presence. She had also made a study of the meaning of dreams and it was this knowledge that helped them to solve the mystery when the husband had a strange dream during his stay.

The dream involved a stuffed crocodile, an old sign representing an apothecary or doctor, and while the man could not explain how or why he should feel this way, he was convinced that the dream was something to do with the unseen woman . . .

The only member of the medical profession whom they had a close association with was a retired woman doctor that the man's wife had met 15 years earlier and had kept in contact with on a fairly regular basis. She had last written to the woman only a month previously but had not yet received a reply. This was strange in itself as she always received a prompt response and she had already become a little concerned. Perhaps it was this concern which led her to associate this old friend with the dream.

On 21st June she telephoned her doctor friend to learn from her housekeeper that her friend had died earlier that month.

# RHOSSILI

## To Claim the Prize Once More . . .

IN the 17th century, the Mansel family of the village of Llanddewi were amongst the most notorious of the many smugglers who operated off the South Wales coastline. Their exploits have become part of the folk-lore of the area, but perhaps one of their greatest moments is re-enacted in a ghostly fashion to this day.

The beach at Rhossili Bay sweeps around from Worms Head to Burry Holms. Still protruding from its final resting place now set deep in the sands of the bay are the wooden ribs of the *Helvetia*, wrecked there in 1887. The Helvetia was by no means the only ship to run aground in the bay, and the area is still today a magnet for those looking to try their luck. Coins and other items are washed up on the beach from time to time even now, particularly after heavy winter storms.

One of the Mansels was the first to reach the famous 'Dollar' ship when it was wrecked on the shore of Rhossili in a heavy storm although it is not recorded whether or not the wrecking was caused by accident or design. He crammed his coach with the Spanish gold liberated from the ship before the lawful owner of the prize, the Lord of the Manor of Rhossili, could claim his rights. Mansel forced his coach and horses on through the driving rain to make good his escape, heavily laden with his booty.

A phantom coach has been seen from time to time, still charging across the sand dunes to claim the prize once more.

This is not the only ghostly presence which continues to bear the mark of the infamous Mansels. The sounds of their battles with their greatest rivals, the Herbert family, have been heard at several bays and beaches around the Gower peninsula.

The Mansel family gained respectability through the generations, and it is a Lady Mansel who is now said to haunt the Old Stradey House on the western edge of Llanelli. It is thought to be her ghostly hands which play the organ music that has been heard coming from one of the thick walls.


## A Persistent Red Lady

ALONG the coastal path between Port Eynon and Rhossili can be found Paviland Cave. In 1823 a skeleton was found in the cave by the Reverend William Buckland, a professor of geology at Oxford University, who dated it as coming from the Romano-British era. The skeleton was headless and stained brick red, possibly because the corpse had been wrapped in red ochre as part of a burial ceremony. At the time it was a most sensational archaeological find.

Shortly after this discovery a number of stories began to emerge about a ghostly red figure, a hideous witch-like crone, which would emerge from the depths of the cave and scream curses from the ledges.

In 1923 the cave was re-excavated and it was discovered at this time that the skeleton could be dated much earlier and belonged to a prehistoric male youth, a Cro-Magnon. Despite this, the tales of the Red Lady persisted.

# ST ATHAN

### A Loving Sister

NEAR the village of St Athan is the site of West Norchete (West Orchard) Castle which was once the home of Sir Jasper Berkerolles. His wife was Lady de Clare, daughter of the Norman Lord of Glamorgan. Berkerolles left his wife for a number of years while he joined a crusade to the Holy Land, and on his return he accused her of having been unfaithful in his absence. She denied the accusation, but he persisted, citing as her lover his neighbour, Sir Gilbert D'Umpherville of East Norchete.

Sir Jasper recalled some of the terrible things he had seen performed by the barbarian hordes in order to exact a punishment on her. He instructed his servants to bury her up to her neck in a field close to the castle. He then commanded that she be denied food and water until she should die of hunger and thirst.

His wife's sister begged Sir Jasper to at least allow her to visit Lady de Clare each day and although he agreed to this it was on the condition that she did not take as much as a drop of water or a crumb of food with her. The visits were made each morning and, while she abided by Berkerolles' orders, she trailed her long dress in the grass of the meadow and collected enough moisture each visit in order to keep her sister alive for ten days.

Shortly after her death his wife's innocence was vindicated and Berkerolles went mad when he realised what he done.

In 1863, women who went milking in the early hours of the morning reported that they had often seen a beautiful lady walking round and round on a certain spot in the meadow, but they could never understand why.

It may have been reasonable to expect that any ghost seen at this site would have been that of the contrite Berkerolles, or his mistreated wife, but it appears that the restless spirit belongs to her dedicated sister who continues to gather dew, long after her own death.

# SOUTHERNDOWN

## The Wrecker Lord of Dunraven Castle

BUILT near Southerndown in the 12th century, Dunraven Castle has gone through continuous rebuilding over the years and by the early 19th century it had been transformed into a large Gothic style castellated mansion.

In the late 17th century, however, the house was the property of the Vaughans, a once wealthy family who had fallen on hard times and became involved in wrecking. By the early 18th century, Walter Vaughan had become so successful at his trade that he became known as 'The Wrecker Lord'. Indeed he had become so skilled in tricking ships onto the rocks of the coast at Southerndown that locals began to claim that he was in fact in league with the devil. Vaughan was certainly unscrupulous in his activities, not only taking the ship's cargo and any valuables found on the bodies of drowned sailors, but also their clothes. Any survivors were murdered by Vaughan's men as soon as they were found.

Walter Vaughan had a son whom he was having educated in mainland Europe. The son was due to return to Dunraven Castle on his 21st birthday. As the date approached Walter Vaughan laid plans to host a lavish party, and he then prepared to wreck another ship in order to pay for the festivities. Winter was approaching and there were plenty of opportunities as many vessels found passage difficult enough in the rough seas off the South Wales coast.

Before too long, Vaughan and his men were successful in luring a ship onto the rocks at Witches Point. On this occasion there were no survivors, saving them the need to finish off their work. Vaughan and his men set about the bodies of the sailors as they were washed up on the beach. On one of the bodies Vaughan found a ring bearing his own family crest. Walter Vaughan had brought about the death of his own son.

Devastated by this, he took to drink and was often to be seen roaming the beach, ranting and raving. Finally he threw himself into the sea and drowned. His ghost is still said to wander the beach in torment, to this day suffering with the guilt he brought on himself.


## The Blue Lady

DUNRAVEN CASTLE is not only host to the ghost of Walter Vaughan, it is also home to the spirit of an unknown lady who appears to pose no threat and yet has the ability to disturb.

During the First World War, the castle was used by the Red Cross as a convalescent home. In April 1917, a nursing sister arrived at the house to join the staff. She was given quarters in what was known as the Amber Room, which was situated on the second floor, overlooking the drive.

The sister was woken one night by a draught on her face and a soft rustling sound. She was about to get out of bed to investigate when she saw the small figure of an old lady wearing a light blue dress walk slowly from the doorway to the fireplace. The nurse turned on the light, but the figure had disappeared, leaving behind an overwhelming odour of mimosa. The nurse thought little of it at the time, believing that perhaps she had been dreaming, but she knew this was not the case when she saw the same figure again later in the year.

In August, the nurse, still quartered in the Amber Room, switched off her bedroom light after reading quite late into the night. Almost immediately, the room was once more filled with the scent of mimosa. The sister looked up and could see in the moonlight the figure of the Blue Lady sitting on a chair beside the fireplace. The nurse, afraid this time, fled straight to a friend's room and stayed with her for the rest of the night.

Several other nurses who stayed in the Amber Room have also reported seeing the ghost of the Blue Lady. On each occasion, her appearances were accompanied by the smell of mimosa.

# SWANBRIDGE

## The Captain's Wife at Sully House

SULLY HOUSE near Swanbridge was once the home of a ship's captain, and on one of his voyages he took the unusual decision that his wife should go with him. During the journey, however, she caught a fever and died. The captain was naturally anxious to keep the news from his crew. They, being a superstitious breed, would not have been happy with the idea of continuing their voyage with a corpse on board the ship. The captain was conscious that it was bad enough, at least as far as the crew were concerned, that he had set sail with a woman.

In order to conceal her death, the captain doubled up his wife's body and placed it in a lead-lined box which he kept in his cabin. For the remainder of the voyage he managed to keep up the pretence that his wife was well despite the fact that she did not appear on deck. '

At the end of the voyage the captain brought the box back to Sully by putting it into a small boat and rowing it ashore. He then placed it first in the cellar of the house and from there moved it to a makeshift grave he had dug in the woods which lay to the rear of the house. The body was to reside there until a proper coffin could be delivered.

When the coffin arrived, the captain and the undertaker returned to the grave only to find that it was empty. The belief was that a member of the crew had followed him ashore, and under the misapprehension that the box contained treasure had decided to steal it. The captain, who was distraught at this turn of events, himself died shortly afterwards.

Soon after the captain's death, stories began to emerge that Sully House and the woods behind it were haunted by the ghost of the dead wife who had been denied a Christian burial. Many people claimed to have seen her travelling from the woods to the house. Sometimes she was seen dressed in white, at other times in black.

Some years later, the then tenant of the house was woken by the screams of a serving maid who had herself woken to find the ghost of the captain's wife standing beside her bed. The maid was so terrified that she gave up her job immediately and left the house rather than spend another night there.

In 1870 some repairs were being made to the stables near the house which required the lifting of a number of flagstones in the yard. Beneath them was found the remains of the captain's wife. It was decided that whoever had disturbed her rest had kept the box for its lead lining, although why her body had not simply been replaced in the woods has not been explained.

A second tale exists concerning a Colonel Rhys who lived in the house at the end of the 18th century. In this tale the Colonel dies in a vicious sword fight with his wife's lover, Henry Winstanley, a young ship's captain. The wife and Winstanley buried the Colonel's body beneath a shrubbery and fled to sea. As in the previous tale, the crew were uncomfortable with the thought of a woman being on board the ship and mutinied. When they brought the ship back to Sully Island they set fire to the ship, leaving the lovers locked in their cabin to perish. The tale ends as the other with sightings of a woman haunting Sully House, sometimes wearing white, sometimes black. It is also claimed that at times screams and shouts have been heard, accompanied by the clash of swords – a re-enactment of that fatal sword fight between

Colonel Rhys and Captain Winstanley.

Sully House is no more, but on that same site now stands a reminder of these stories, a restaurant called 'The Captain's Wife'.

# SWANSEA

### Ghostly Happenings at the Grand Theatre

THE Grand Theatre in Swansea was originally opened in 1897 by the then world famous soprano Dame Adelina Patti. Dame Patti had already come to live in South Wales at Craig-y-Nos in the Swansea valley. The 1980s saw the theatre go through major reconstruction work, giving it one of the most modern exteriors in the city centre. Inside, however, most of the original splendour of the theatre has been retained and indeed much of it enhanced. Another element of the theatre that has not been disposed of is the ghostly figure of a White Lady who has been sighted many times over the years.

One candidate for the possible identity of the ghost is a young actress remembered only as Jenny. This young woman gave her last performance at the Grand Theatre in 1911 immediately prior to leaving for America aboard the ill-fated ship, the *SS Titanic*. The most popular belief, however, is that the ghost belongs to Adelina Patti herself.

In 1972, the actress Eleanor Thomas, who later became wardrobe mistress at the Grand Theatre, saw the ghost of the White Lady while she was appearing in a production of *A Streetcar named Desire*. During a performance her eye was caught by a figure in the dress circle who was wearing a dress of dazzling white. At first she found the brightness of her appearance to be a distraction, but even as she looked at the figure it disappeared. When she reported the strange event to Vivyan Ellacott, who was the house manager, she discovered that he too had seen the White Lady but had previously kept quiet.

The ghost was quiet during the restoration of the building but she returned once more when most of the work was over. The White Lady re-appeared during a performance of *Babes in the Wood* which was being put on as the theatre's annual pantomime. Wendy Weaver, who was playing the Fairy Godmother, was standing alone in the wings waiting to make her entrance, and while she waited there she became aware of a presence at her side. As she watched for the cue to make her entrance onto the stage she felt a cold hand rest on her shoulder. When she realised that there was no one with her, she understandably became afraid. Perhaps the ghost had sensed approaching stage fright, for all the hand did was lead her onto the stage, right on cue.

In February 1984, with reports of the return of the ghost increasing, the *South Wales Evening Post* arranged an all night vigil. They sent a reporter, Antony Harris, and a photographer, Ian Kennedy, to spend the night in the theatre and to record their experiences. In his report, Harris described the events of the night as harrowing.

It is obvious from Harris's report that both he and Kennedy were feeling quite nervous even as the night began and by 1.20 am nerves were starting to get a little frayed. They heard noises from the bar which sounded like bottles being clinked together. At 2.25 am Harris recorded that the temperature started to drop suddenly. Even more disturbingly, half an hour later they were subjected to the sound of a woman crying. Neither of them could believe quite what they were experiencing, but just as suddenly as it had begun the crying stopped. For the next three hours they were terrorised by a series of sounds, giving them one fright after another. First there was the sound of footsteps, then that of a harp being strummed by a single finger, and finally a strange, soft music.

At 5 am they took refuge in one of the theatre's four boxes and huddled together like children. There they felt that perhaps this confined space offered some form of sanctuary. A protection from whatever it was that was stalking the theatre.

A month later, a theatre electrician confessed that he had concealed himself in one of the lighting boxes and had been responsible for some of the noises such as the bottles clinking. He had left shortly after that, but Antony Harris is still convinced that the electrician could not have been responsible for all that he and Kennedy felt and heard during that night.

The increase in the level of interest generated in the White Lady led to TV AM holding a seance in the theatre. The medium hired for the occasion made no claims of direct contact with any spirits during the seance, but indicated that there was some sort of presence in the dress circle.

Although the medium could not have known it, this was the same spot where Eleanor Thomas had first seen the ghostly White Lady in 1972.


## A Prank in Cwmdonkin Park

IT is thought by many that the ghost of Dylan Thomas haunts the Old Boathouse at Laugharne in Dyfed where he worked. If this is not the case then certainly his legacy permeates the building. It is also possible that his spirit has returned to an earlier home.

Margaret Hopkins was introduced to Dylan Thomas in 1939 while in the company of a mutual friend and although she met him only once he left a lasting impression on her.

In 1973 she was sitting on a bench in Cwmdonkin Park, Swansea, close to Cwmdonkin Terrace where Dylan had grown up. Suddenly she was showered in a rain of stones, twigs and turf from the sloping bank behind her but when she looked around there was no one in sight. A gardener working nearby neither saw nor heard anything of the incident. While it would be easy to dismiss this as a prank by children who had succeeded in avoiding detection, Margaret was left with the strong impression that it was Dylan himself playing a joke on her.

Dylan Thomas wrote a poem about a hunchback sitting in the same park, perhaps even sitting on the same bench. The hunchback too was pelted with stones.

# TINTERN ABBEY

## A Soldier's Request

THE ruins of the 12th-century Cistercian abbey at Tintern provided inspiration for Wordsworth and it has been a regular stop on the tourist route ever since.

Shortly before the turn of the century, a man and his wife visited the ruins while on a cycling holiday. It was already late and the scene was moonlit. The lady claimed to have psychic powers and showed no signs of concern or fear when her right hand seemed to gain a life of its own, rapping several times on her knee. Calmly she asked if there was someone there who wanted to communicate with her. She also asked that if that was so then could the message be given with less force, and by use of the usual manner, being one tap for 'no' and three taps for 'yes'.

By this method and without the trappings of a glass and a lettered board, a message was gathered by the long-winded method of going through the alphabet until she felt three taps.

After a considerable length of time the couple had learned the ghost's predicament. It was the spirit of a soldier who had died close to the abbey while fighting in the service of Henry II. The soldier had been buried nearby without ceremony. No prayers had ever been said over his body and until two Masses were said in his name his spirit would be unable to rest.

The couple asked in return how the soldier had come to seek their assistance after so many years. They found it particularly intriguing that they, a pair of Anglicans whose church did not include prayers for the dead, should be asked for this service. The ghost replied that he had tried many times to contact both his own descendants and other visitors to the area, but previously without success. The difference in religion was seen as of no consequence so long as the Masses were said. When the couple promised that this would be done the spirit left them.

The following night the couple returned to the same spot and again the woman's hand became controlled by the ghost who repeated his request.

A few days later, when the couple had returned to

London, they were met by a Catholic clergyman who was also a family friend. They had written to him from Tintern and explained the circumstances to him. The clergyman, being of an open mind, agreed to say not two but four Masses for the soldier.

The incident was forgotten until some ten years later, in November 1905, when the couple attended a seance. On this occasion the message was received, 'Very many thanks for the Masses said.'

Afterwards, the two women who had sat on either side of the woman who had taken part in that earlier communication swore they had seen the bearded figure of a handsome man standing behind her.

# TONGWYNLAIS

## Greenmeadow's Legacy

ORIGINALLY a 17th century farmhouse by the name of Pantgwynlais, Greenmeadow was a large, atmospheric mansion on the edge of Tongwynlais. The house was the home of the Lewis family for over 100 years and by the early 19th century had become the property of Wyndham Lewis, Member of Parliament for Glamorgan Boroughs. In the year he took ownership an imposing façade was added to the front of the building and it was renamed Greenmeadow by his wife, Mary Anne Lewis. After Lewis's death in 1838, the property attracted its first hint of notoriety, not for any aspect of the paranormal but because Lewis's political colleague Benjamin Disraeli openly conducted a romantic relationship with the young widow. It was widely suspected that the two had been involved for some time prior to Wyndham Lewis's death. This suspicion certainly seemed to be vindicated when they were married less than a year later. The property was then inherited by Wyndham's younger brother, Henry.

Over the ensuing years, several sightings were recorded of the ghost of a man, and although two of the sightings were 18 years apart they do have something in common. Although the two sightings appear to relate to different ghosts they may well be the same one – other sightings have described apparitions which fall between the two extremes. Perhaps this ghost is able to manifest itself at different stages in its life. The ghost was described in 1848 by Martha Moggridge of Rhiwbina as a small old man in a green coat and white knee breeches, with a silver rapier hanging from a sash. The apparition entered the bedroom where Martha was sitting with her sister and then moved from one side of the room to the other, constantly tapping on the wall. Suddenly he threw his arms in the air in a gesture of great despair and disappeared.

In 1886 a sighting was made by a Captain Mostyn, a hero of Rourke's Drift. He claimed to have seen a tall red-haired man leaning on a sword and looking out of the window when suddenly the figure dropped its sword, fell to its knees as if to pray, then vanished.

Eventually the property fell into disrepair and in 1940 part of the building collapsed, killing two men when it did so. Tales of ghosts seemed to have died away by this time, and it remained like this for over 30 years.

By 1974 the house had been demolished and a small council estate built on its site. Mrs Suzanne Morgan lived in a four bedroomed house on the estate with her eight children. She reported that on several occasions she and the children had seen the ghost of an old woman in one of the upstairs rooms. She also complained of taps being turned on in the bathroom while she and the children slept. Loud banging noises were heard coming from the attic, followed immediately by the sound of heavy footsteps. Regularly the family would get up in the morning to find ash had been spilled from the fireplace and raked into the carpet. Instead of these manifestations fading away over time they escalated both in frequency and in their ability to disturb. Furniture began to be moved, and one day the ghost of the old woman appeared on the landing and called out 'Julie'. This was the name of one of the children, and from that moment they no longer felt able to sleep in the bedrooms and took to sleeping downstairs instead.

As news of the haunting became known, the *Cardiff Leader* investigated by sending a reporter and photographer to spend a night in the house. On the designated night, Mrs Morgan and her children took to their beds downstairs while the two men settled down for the night in two armchairs in one of the bedrooms.

Nothing happened until two in the morning when it grew strangely cold and a haze seemed to fill the room. The rest of the night passed without incident. Before leaving the room, the photographer decided to shoot a roll of film in case there was anything which could not normally be seen by the human eye. When the film was developed, however, it was found to be unexposed. It had been reeled through the camera normally and yet it remained blank. The camera was examined closely for any faults but none could be found.

The two o'clock haze could have been explained away by the fact that both men smoked, but the non-exposure of the film is not so easy to understand.

The facts of this case were passed on to the editors of *Psychic News* for their opinions. Their conclusion was that the phenomena could have been caused by the activities of a poltergeist.

Locals have no doubt that this was the legacy of Greenmeadow.

# USK

## A Haunted Room

IN 1958, the Cross Keys Inn in Usk gained more than a little media coverage when its then landlord, Roland Hoffman, claimed that one of the rooms was haunted. Hoffman reported that the door latch to room 3 would rise and fall of its own accord and that the door would then open and close, seemingly without anyone passing through it.

The story lead to a television camera crew conducting a vigil in the room at night, using only a single candle for light. In the early hours of the morning the candle blew out, apparently without cause. The crew, feeling a mixture of excitement and trepidation, waited a little while then relit the candle. It was blown out again but when they lit it a third time it continued to burn. The crew had nothing more to report for the night-long wait.

It was later discovered that the inn had once been a hospice attached to Usk Priory and that in the 17th century a monk had been martyred nearby. The unfortunate man had also been hung, drawn and quartered. It was assumed from this revelation that it was the ghost of the monk who haunted room 3.

Subsequent landlords have put forward an alternative theory about the identity of the ghost. They claim that it may be the spirit of a 16 year old girl who had once committed suicide at the inn.

# A GLOSSARY OF DEATH OMENS

## Canwyll Corff – Corpse Candles

The sight of Canwyll Corff is an even more dreaded event than the other omens as it is seen outside a house where someone will die that night. It appears as either a single or a series of blue flickering flames, and at times, though less frequently, these lights enact a macabre funeral march to the site of the forthcoming burying. Folklore has it that sometimes this procession is headed by a spectral manifestation of the person who is about to die.

## Cwm Annwn – The Dogs of Darkness

These are the black dogs of Satan who hunt for lost souls for their master. They are also said to be omens of impending disaster.

## Cyhyraeth

This is a warning of news of death, which this time comes in the form of a wailing sound heard by a close friend or relative who will shortly hear the bad news. If the wailing is heard near the sea it is an indication of a fatal shipwreck.

## Deryn Corff – The Corpse Bird

Although less frequently reported than other omens, the Deryn Corff, a large black bird, appears at night perched on a wall beside a house where someone will die that night. Sometimes it calls loudly, 'Dewch, dewch' (Come, come).

## Dog of Death

Unlike the Cwm Annwn who are always black, the Dog of Death is always white. The dog stands outside the house of the dying person and howls.

## Gwrach y Rhibyn – The Hag of the Mist

Although usually taking the appearance of a woman, a Gwrach y Rhibyn may also appear as a man. The creature has long, skinny arms, straggly hair and black fangs. The Gwrach may also have huge leathery wings, or use a cloak to aid it in flight. It is most likely to visit a house if someone inside is dying, and although it will remain outside it will beat its wings against the window and call out the name of the dying person.

## Tolaeth

This is a knocking or rapping sound which warns of impending death, or news of a death.

# BIBLIOGRAPHY

*Welsh Ghostly Encounters* Jane Pugh, 1990
*The Haunting of Gwent & Glamorgan* Russell Gascoine, 1993
*Lord Halifax's Ghost Book* Lord Halifax, 1937
*Ghosts & Legends of Wales* J.A. Brooks, 1987
*Ghosts & Legends of the Vale of Neath* Alun Evans & William Willis, 1987
*British Goblins* Wirt Sikes, 1880
*Theatre Ghosts* Roy Harley Lewis, 1988
*Ghosts, Legends and Lore of Wales* P.H. Jeffery, 1990
*Haunted Gwent* Alan Roderick, 1995
*Welsh Folk Tales* Robin Gwyndaf, 1992

# INDEX